Noreen. When my
Dad passed away... my
girlfriend gave this book
& it help me to go
through the loss. I hope
it will help yo too.

Thinking of you!

Martha

LOVE REMEMBERED

A BOOK OF COMFORT
IN GRIEF

Bereavement is the deepest initiation into the mysteries of
human life, an initiation more searching and profound
than even happy love. Love remembered and consecrated
by grief belongs to the eternal world.

Dean W.R. Inge, after the death of his daughter

A lily of a day,
Is fairer far in May,
Although it fall and die that night–
It was the plant and flower of light.

Ben Jonson

LOVE REMEMBERED

A BOOK OF COMFORT IN GRIEF

He is made one with Nature: there is heard
His voice in all her music, from the moan
Of thunder, to the song of night's sweet bird;
He is a presence to be felt and known
In darkness and in light…

Percy Bysshe Shelley

Celia Haddon

Michael Joseph
LONDON

MICHAEL JOSEPH LTD

Published by the Penguin Group
27 Wrights Lane, London W8 5TZ
Viking Penguin Inc., 375 Hudson Street, New York, New York 10014, USA
Penguin Books Australia Ltd, Ringwood, Victoria, Australia
Penguin Books Canada Ltd, 10 Alcorn Avenue, Toronto, Ontario, Canada M4V 3B2
Penguin Books (NZ) Ltd, 182–190 Wairu Road, Aukland 10, New Zealand

Penguin Books Ltd, Registered Offices: Harmondsworth, Middlesex, England

First published 1997
1 3 5 7 9 10 8 6 4 2

Typeset in 11/12pt Goudy
Manufactured in China by Imago Publishing Ltd
Design and computer page make-up by Penny Mills

A CIP catalogue record for this book is available from the British Library

ISBN 0 7181 4120 2

The moral right of the author has been asserted

In memory of my mother,
the painter Joyce Haddon.

Love's not Time's fool, though rosy lips and cheeks
Within his bending sickle's compass come;
Love alters not with his brief hours and weeks,
But bears it out even to the edge of doom.

WILLIAM SHAKESPEARE

IF IT MUST BE …

If it must be
You speak no more with us,
Nor smile no more with us,
Nor walk no more with us,
Then let us take a patience and a calm.
For even now the green leaf explodes,
Sun lightens stone, and all the river burns.

ANONYMOUS

CONTENTS

The time will come when all that is precious in the past will come up to us again. It is on the way even now to those that try to *live*.

GEORGE MACDONALD
Letter 1889

IMMORTALITIES

Love is a great matter, in very truth a great good; which alone maketh everything that is heavy, light; and beareth equally unequal burdens. For it carrieth a burden without a burden, and maketh every thing that is bitter, sweet and delightsome....

Nothing is sweeter than love, nothing stronger, nothing higher, nothing more ample, nothing more pleasant, nothing fuller nor better in heaven or in earth: for that love has his beginning from God, and cannot rest but in God above all creatures.

He that loveth, flieth, runneth and rejoiceth; he is free and not held in. He giveth all for all, and hath all in all.... Love oftentimes knoweth no measure, but inflameth above all measure. Love feeleth no burden, weigheth not pains, desireth above its strength, complaineth not of impossibility, for that it thinketh all things lawful and possible. It is therefore able to undertake all things, and performeth and bringeth many things to effect; whereas he that doth not love, fainteth and can do nothing.

Love always watcheth, and sleeping sleepeth not, being wearied is not tired; straitened is not pressed; frighted, is not troubled; but like a lively flame and burning torch, breaketh upwards, and passeth through all with great security....

Love is swift, sincere, pious, sweet and delightful, strong, patient, faithful, prudent, suffering, full of courage, and never seeking itself. For where one seeketh himself, there he falleth from love. Love is ... devout and thankful unto God, trusting and hoping always in him, even then when God imparteth no sweetness unto it: for without sorrow none liveth in love.

St Thomas à Kempis

Do not stand at my grave and weep.
I am not there, I do not sleep.
I am a thousand winds that blow.
I am diamond glints on snow.
I am the sunlight on ripened grain.
I am the gentle autumn rain.
When you awaken in the morning's hush,
I am the swift uplifting rush
Of quiet birds in circled flight.
I am the soft stars that shine at night.
Do not stand at my grave and cry,
I am not there; I did not die.

AUTHOR UNKNOWN.

A poem left for his parents by Stephen Cummins,
who was killed by a terrorist bomb in 1989

WE GIVE THEM BACK

We seem to give them back to Thee, O God, who gavest them to us. Yet, as Thou didst not lose them in giving, so do we not lose them by their return. Not as the world giveth, givest Thou, O Lover of souls. What Thou givest, Thou takest not away, for what is Thine is ours also, if we are Thine. And life is eternal and love is immortal, and death is only an horizon, and an horizon is nothing save the limit of our sight. Lift us up, strong Son of God, that we may see further: cleanse our eyes that we may see more clearly: draw us closer to Thyself that we may know ourselves to be nearer to our loved ones who are with Thee. And while Thou dost prepare a place for us, prepare us also for that happy place, that where Thou art, we may be also for evermore.

Fr Bede Jarrett, O. P.

HEAVEN-HAVEN

I have desired to go
  Where springs not fail,
To fields where flies no sharp and sided hail
  And a few lilies blow.

And I have asked to be
  Where no storms come,
Where the green swell is in the havens dumb,
  And out of the swing of the sea.

GERARD MANLEY HOPKINS

A LAST MESSAGE FROM THE ONE WE LOVED

Death is nothing at all. It does not count. I have only slipped away into the next room. Nothing has happened. Everything remains exactly as it was. I am I, and you are you, and the old life we lived so fondly together is untouched, unchanged. Whatever we were to each other, that we are still. Call me by the old familiar name. Speak of me in the easy way which you always used. Put no difference into your tone. Wear no forced air of solemnity or sorrow. Laugh as we always laughed at the little jokes that we enjoyed together. Play, smile, think of me, pray for me. Let my name be ever the household word that it always was. Life means all that it ever meant. It is the same as it ever was. There is absolute and unbroken continuity. What is this death but a negligible accident? Why should I be out of mind because I am out of sight? I am waiting for you, for an interval, somewhere very near, just round the corner. All is well. Nothing is hurt; nothing is lost. One brief moment and all will be as it was before. How we shall laugh at the trouble of parting when we meet again!

HENRY SCOTT HOLLAND

A CHERUB WHO HAD LOST HIS WAY

He did but float a little way
Adown the stream of time;
With dreamy eyes watching the ripples play,
Or listening their fairy chime.
His slender sail
Ne'er felt the gale;
He did but float a little way,
And, putting to the shore
While yet 'twas early day,
Went calmly on his way,
To dwell with us no more!
No jarring did he feel,
No grating on his vessel's keel;
A strip of yellow sand
Mingled the waters with the land,
Where he was seen no more:
O stern word – Nevermore!
Full short his journey was; no dust
Of earth into his sandals clave;
The weary weight that old men must,
He bore not to the grave.
He seemed a cherub who had lost his way
And wandered hither, so his stay
With us was short, and 'twas most meet
That he should be no delver in earth's clod,
Nor need to pause and cleanse his feet
To stand before his God:
O blest word – Evermore!

JAMES RUSSELL LOWELL

CROSSING THE WORLD

They that love beyond the world cannot be separated by it.

Death cannot kill what never dies. Nor can spirits ever be divided that love and live in the same divine principle; the root and record of their friendship.

If absence be not death, neither is it theirs.

Death is but crossing the world, as friends do the seas; they live in one another still.

For they must needs be present that love and live in that which is omnipresent.

In this divine glass they see face to face; and their converse is free, as well as pure. This is the comfort of friends, that though they may be said to die, yet their friendship and society are, in the best sense, ever present, because immortal.

WILLIAM PENN

REMEMBER

Remember me when I am gone away,
  Gone far away into the silent land;
  When you can no more hold me by the hand,
Nor I half turn to go yet turning stay.
Remember me when no more day by day
  You tell me of our future that you planned:
  Only remember me; you understand
It will be late to counsel then or pray.
But if you should forget me for a while
  And afterwards remember, do not grieve:
  For if the darkness and corruption leave
  A vestige of the thoughts that once I had,
Better by far you should forget and smile
  Than that you should remember and be sad.

CHRISTINA ROSSETTI

THE SHIP

I am standing on the sea shore. A ship sails and spreads her white sails to the morning breeze and starts for the ocean. She is an object of beauty and I stand watching her till at last she fades on the horizon, and someone at my side says, 'She is gone.'

Gone where? Gone from my sight, that is all; she is just as large in the masts, hull and spars as she was when I saw her, and just as able to bear her load of living freight to its destination.

The diminished size and total loss of sight is in me, not in her; and just at the moment when someone at my side says, 'She is gone', there are others who are watching her coming, and other voices take up a glad shout, 'There she comes'. And that is Dying.

BISHOP CHARLES BRENT

And do you think, that an unvisited grave, a withered tree, a faded flower or two, are tokens of forgetfulness or cold neglect? Do you think there are no deeds far away from here, in which these dead may be best remembered? There may be people busy in the world at this instance, in whose good actions and good thoughts these very graves - neglected at they look to us - are the chief instruments.

There is nothing, no, nothing innocent or good, that dies, and is forgotten. Let us hold to that faith, or none. An infant, a prattling child, dying in its cradle, will live again in the better thoughts of those who loved it; and play its part, through them, in the redeeming actions of the world, though its body be burned to ashes or drowned in the deepest sea. There is not an angel added to the Host of Heaven but does its blessed work on earth in those that loved it here. Forgotten! oh, if the good deeds of human creatures could be traced to their source, how beautifully would even death appear; for how much charity, mercy, and purified affection would be seen to have their growth in dusty graves.

CHARLES DICKENS

GRIEFS

Dark house, by which once more I stand
  Here in the long unlovely street,
  Doors, where my heart was used to beat
So quickly, waiting for a hand,

A hand that can be clasp'd no more -
  Behold me, for I cannot sleep,
  And like a guilty thing I creep
At earliest morning to the door.

He is not here; but far away
  The noise of life begins again,
  And ghastly thro' the drizzling rain
On the bald street breaks the blank day.

ALFRED, LORD TENNYSON

SONG

Stop all the clocks, cut off the telephone,
Prevent the dog from barking with a juicy bone,
Silence the pianos and with muffled drum
Bring out the coffin, let the mourners come.

Let aeroplanes circle moaning overhead
Scribbling on the sky the message He Is Dead,
Put crêpe bows round the white necks of the public doves,
Let the traffic policemen wear black cotton gloves.

He was my North, my South, my East and West,
My working week and my Sunday rest,
My noon, my midnight, my talk, my song;
I thought that love would last for ever: I was wrong.

The stars are not wanted now; put out every one:
Pack up the moon and dismantle the sun;
Pour away the ocean and sweep up the woods:
For nothing now can ever come to any good.

W.H. AUDEN

WHERE IS GOD?

Meanwhile, where is God? This is one of the most disquieting symptoms. When you are happy, so happy that you have no sense of needing Him, so happy that you are tempted to feel His claims upon you as an interruption, if you remember yourself and turn to Him with gratitude and praise, you will be – or so it feels – welcomed with open arms. But go to Him when your need is desperate, when all other help is vain, and what do you find? A door slammed in your face, and a sound of bolting and double bolting on the inside. After that, silence. You may as well turn away. The longer you wait, the more emphatic the silence will become. There are no lights in the windows. It might be an empty house. Was it ever inhabited? It seemed so once. And that seeming was as strong as this. What can this mean? Why is He so present a commander in our time of prosperity and so very absent a help in time of trouble?

I tried to put some of these thoughts to C. this afternoon. He reminded me that the same thing seems to have happened to Christ: "Why has thou forsaken me?" I know. Does that make it easier to understand?

C.S. LEWIS

THEY ARE ALL GONE
INTO THE WORLD OF LIGHT

They are all gone into the world of light!
   And I alone sit lingering here;
Their very memory is fair and bright,
   And my sad thoughts doth clear.

It glows and glitters in my cloudy breast,
   Like stars upon some gloomy grove,
Or those faint beams in which this hill is dressed,
   After the sun's remove.

I see them walking in an air of glory,
   Whose light doth trample on my days:
My days, which are at best but dull and hoary,
   Mere glimmerings and decays.

Oh holy hope, and high humility,
   High as the heavens above!
These are your walks, and you have showed them me,
   To kindle my cold love.

Dear, beauteous death! the jewel of the just,
   Shining nowhere but in the dark;
What mysteries do lie beyond thy dust,
   Could man outlook that mark!

He that hath found some fledged bird's nest may know
   At first sight if the bird be flown;
But what fair well or grove he sings in now,
   That is to him unknown.

And yet, as angels in some brighter dreams
   Call to the soul when man doth sleep,
So some strange thoughts transcend our wonted themes
   And into glory peep.

If a star were confined into a tomb,
　Her captive flames must needs burn there;
But when the hand that locked her up gives room,
　She'll shine through all the sphere.

O Father of eternal life, and all
　Created glories under Thee!
Resume Thy spirit from this world of thrall
　Into true liberty!

Either disperse these mists, which blot and fill
　My pèrspective (still) as they pass,
Or else remove me hence unto that hill,
　Where I shall need no glass.

Henry Vaughan

A MOTHER'S DEATH

The life which made my own life pleasant is at an end, and the gates of death are shut upon my prospects. The loss of a friend upon whom the heart was fixed, to whom every wish and endeavour tended, is a state of dreary desolation, in which the mind looks abroad impatient of itself, and finds nothing but emptiness and horror....

These are the calamities by which Providence gradually disengages us from the love of life. Other evils fortitude may repel, or hope may mitigate; but irreparable privation leaves nothing to exercise resolution or flatter expectation. The dead cannot return, and nothing is left us here but languishment and grief.

Yet such is the course of nature, that whoever lives long must outlive those whom he loves and honours. Such is the condition of our present existence, that life must one time lose its associations, and every inhabitant of the earth must walk downward to the grave, alone and unregarded, without any partner of his joy or grief, without any interested witness of his misfortunes or success....

We know little of the state of departed souls, because such knowledge is not necessary to a good life. Reason deserts us at the brink of the grave, and can give no further intelligence. Revelation is not wholly silent. There is joy in the angels of Heaven over one sinner that repenteth; and surely this joy is not incommunicable to souls disentangled from the body, and made like angels.

Let hope therefore dictate ... that the union of souls may still remain; and that we who are struggling with sin, sorrow, and infirmities, may have our part in the attention and kindness of those who have finished their course, and are now receiving their reward.

SAMUEL JOHNSON

MY DEAREST DUST

My dearest dust, could not thy hasty day
Afford thy drousy patience leave to stay
One hour longer: so we might either
Sat up, or gone to bed together?
But since thy finished labour hath possest
Thy weary limbs with early rest,
Enjoy it sweetly: and thy widow-bride
Shall soon repose her by thy slumbering
    side.
Whose business, now, is only to prepare
My nightly dress, and call to prayer:
Mine eyes wax heavy and ye day grows old.
The dew falls thick, my belov'd grows cold.
Draw, draw ye closed curtains: and make
    room:
My dear, my dearest dust: I come, I come.

LADY CATHERINE DYER

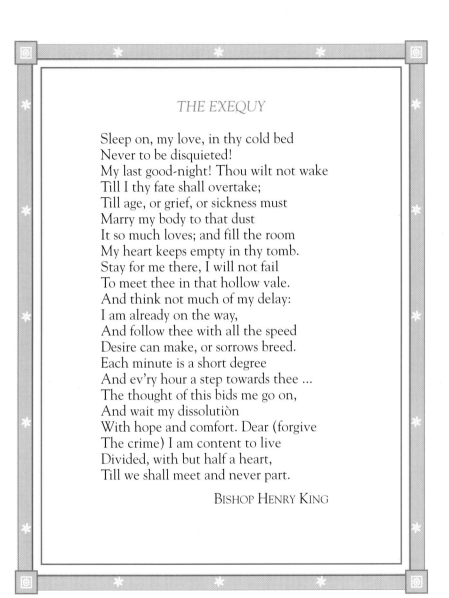

THE EXEQUY

Sleep on, my love, in thy cold bed
Never to be disquieted!
My last good-night! Thou wilt not wake
Till I thy fate shall overtake;
Till age, or grief, or sickness must
Marry my body to that dust
It so much loves; and fill the room
My heart keeps empty in thy tomb.
Stay for me there, I will not fail
To meet thee in that hollow vale.
And think not much of my delay:
I am already on the way,
And follow thee with all the speed
Desire can make, or sorrows breed.
Each minute is a short degree
And ev'ry hour a step towards thee ...
The thought of this bids me go on,
And wait my dissolutiòn
With hope and comfort. Dear (forgive
The crime) I am content to live
Divided, with but half a heart,
Till we shall meet and never part.

BISHOP HENRY KING

41

COURAGE AND ENDURANCE

Put forth thy leaf, thou lofty plane,
East wind and frost are safely gone;
With zephyr mild and balmy rain,
The summer comes serenely on;
Earth, air, and sun and skies combine
To promise all that's kind and fair;
But thou, O human heart of mine,
Be still, contain thyself, and bear.

December days were brief and chill,
The winds of March were wild and drear,
And, nearing and receding still,
Spring never would, we thought, be here.
The leaves that burst, the suns that shine,
Had, not the less, their certain date;
And thou, O human heart of mine,
Be still, refrain thyself, and wait.

ARTHUR HUGH CLOUGH

I WILL TRUST

God has created me to do him some definite service. He has committed some work to me which he has not committed to another. I have my mission. I may never know it in this life, but I shall be told it in the next.

I am a link in a chain, a bond of connection between persons. He has not created me for naught. I shall do good. I shall do his work. I shall be an angel of peace, a preacher of truth in my own place while not intending it – if I do but keep his commandments.

Therefore I will trust him. Whatever, wherever I am. I can never be thrown away. If I am in sickness, my sickness may serve him; in perplexity, my perplexity may serve him; if I am in sorrow, my sorrow may serve him. He does nothing in vain. He knows what he is about. He may take away my friends, he may throw me among strangers. He may make me feel desolate, make my spirits sink, hide my future from me – still he knows what he is about.

JOHN HENRY NEWMAN

NOT TO YIELD

Death closes all: but something ere the end,
Some work of noble note, may yet be done,
Not unbecoming men that strove with Gods.
The lights begin to twinkle from the rocks:
The long day wanes: the slow moon climbs: the deep
Moans round with many voices. Come, my friends,
'Tis not too late to seek a newer world.
Push off, and sitting well in order smite
The sounding furrows; for my purpose holds
To sail beyond the sunset, and the baths
Of all the western stars, until I die.
It may be that the gulfs will wash us down:
It may be we shall touch the Happy Isles,
And see the great Achilles, whom we knew.
Tho' much is taken, much abides; and tho'
We are not now that strength which in old days
Moved earth and heaven; that which we are, we are;
One equal temper of heroic hearts,
Made weak by time and fate, but strong in will
To strive, to seek, to find, and not to yield.

ALFRED, LORD TENNYSON

THE POET REMEMBERS HIS DEAD DAUGHTER

Surprised by joy – impatient as the Wind
I turned to share the transport – Oh! with whom
But thee, deep buried in the silent tomb,
That spot which no vicissitude can find?
Love, faithful love, recalled thee to my mind –
But how could I forget thee? Through what power,
Even for the least division of an hour,
Have I been so beguiled as to be blind
To my most grievous loss! That thought's return
Was the worst pang that sorrow ever bore,
Save one, one only, when I stood forlorn,
Knowing my heart's best treasure was no more;
That neither present time, nor years unborn
Could to my sight that heavenly face restore.

WILLIAM WORDSWORTH

DEATH SETS A THING SIGNIFICANT

Death sets a Thing significant
The Eye had hurried by
Except a perished Creature
Entreat us tenderly

To ponder little Workmanships
In Crayon, or in Wool,
With "This was last Her fingers did" –
Industrious until –

The Thimble weighed too heavy –
The stitches stopped – themselves –
And then 'twas put among the Dust
Upon the Closet shelves –

A Book I have – a friend gave –
Whose Pencil – here and there –
Had notched the place that pleased Him –
At Rest – His fingers are –

Now – when I read – I read not –
For interrupting Tears –
Obliterate the Etchings
Too Costly for Repairs

EMILY DICKINSON

NOBLE EFFORTS

I do think that the necessity for exertion, for some kind of action (bodily or mentally) in time of distress, is a most infinite blessing, although the first efforts at such seasons are painful. Something to be done implies that there is yet home of some good thing to be accomplished; or some additional evil that may be avoided, and by degrees the hope absorbs much of the sorrow. It is the woes that cannot in any earthly way be escaped, that admit least earthly comforting ...

There are stages in the contemplation and endurance of great sorrow, which endow men with the same earnestness, and clearness of thought, that in some of old took the form of prophecy. To those who have large capability of loving and suffering, united with great power of firm endurance, there comes a time in their woe, when they are lifted out of the contemplation of their individual case into the searching inquiry into the nature of their calamity, and that remedy (if remedy there be) which may prevent its recurrence to others as well as to themselves. Hence the beautiful, noble efforts which are from time to time brought to light, as being continuously made by those who have once hung on the cross of agony, in order that others may not suffer as they have done; one of the grandest ends which sorrow can accomplish. The sufferer wrestling with God's messenger until a blessing is left behind, not for one alone, but for generations.

ELIZABETH GASKELL

THE TWENTY-THIRD PSALM

The Lord is my shepherd; I shall not want.

He maketh me to lie down in green pastures: he leadeth me beside the still waters.

He restoreth my soul: he leadeth me in the paths of righteousness for his name's sake.

Yea, though I walk through the valley of the shadow of death, I will fear no evil: for thou art with me; thy rod and thy staff they comfort me.

Thou preparest a table before me in the presence of mine enemies: thou anointest my head with oil; my cup runneth over.

Surely goodness and mercy shall follow me all the days of my life: and I will dwell in the house of the Lord for ever.

A REMINDER

If I should die and leave you here awhile,
Be not like others, sore undone, who keep
Long vigils by the silent dust and weep.
For my sake turn again to life and smile,
Nerving thy heart and trembling hand to do
Something to comfort weaker hearts than thine.
Complete these dear unfinished tasks of mine,
And I, perchance, may therein comfort you!

A. PRICE HUGHES

56

CONSOLATIONS

I believe that the wisest plan of bearing sorrow is sometimes not to try to bear it – as long as one is not crippled for one's everyday duties – but to give way to sorrow, utterly and freely. Perhaps sorrow is sent that we *may* give way to it, and, in drinking the cup to the dregs, find some medicine in it itself which we should not find if we began doctoring ourselves, or letting others doctor us....

I write to you because every expression of human sympathy brings some little comfort, if it be only to remind such as you that you are not alone in the world. I know nothing can make up for such a loss as yours. But you will still have love on earth all round you; and *his* love is not dead. It lives still in the next world for you, and perhaps with you. For why should not those who are gone, if they are gone to their Lord, be actually nearer us, not further from us, in the heavenly world, praying for us, and it may be, influencing and guiding us in a hundred ways, of which we in our prison-house of mortality cannot dream.

Yes, do not be afraid to believe that he whom you have loved is still near you, and you near him....

CHARLES KINGSLEY

MARCUS STONE.

DO NOT BE AFRAID

Do not be afraid, for I have redeemed you.
I have called you by your name;
you are mine.

When you walk through the waters, I'll be
with you;
you will never sink beneath the waves.

When the fire is burning all around you,
you will never be consumed by the flames.

When the fear of loneliness is looming,
then remember I am at your side.

You are mine, O my child; I am your Father,
and I love you with a perfect love.

GERARD MARKLAND
from *Isaiah 43*

SORROW COMES IN GREAT WAVES

I don't know *why* we live – the gift of life comes to us from I don't know what source or for what purpose; but I believe we can go on living for the reason that (always up to a certain point) life is the most valuable thing we know anything about, and it is therefore presumptively a great mistake to surrender it while there is any yet left in the cup ... We all live together, and those of us who love and know, live so most. We help each other – even unconsciously, each in our own effort, we lighten the effort of others, we contribute to the sum of success, make it possible for others to live. Sorrow comes in great waves – no one can know that better than you – but it rolls over us, and though it may almost smother us it leaves us on the spot, and we know that if it is strong we are stronger, inasmuch as it passes and we remain. It wears us, uses us, but we wear it and use it in return; and it is blind, whereas we after a manner see ... You are passing through a darkness in which I myself in my ignorance see nothing but that you have been made wretchedly ill by it; but it is only a darkness, it is not an end, or *the* end. Don't think, don't feel, any more than you can help, don't conclude or decide – don't do anything but *wait*....

HENRY JAMES

RESIGNATION

There is no flock, however watched and tended,
But one dead lamb is there!
There is no fireside, howsoe'er defended,
But has one vacant chair!...

Let us be patient! These severe afflictions
Not from the ground arise
But oftentimes celestial benedictions
Assume this dark disguise.

We see but dimly through the mists and vapors;
Amid these earthly damps,
What seem to us but sad, funeral tapers
May be heaven's distant lamps.

There is no Death! What seems so is transition.
This life of mortal breath
Is but a suburb of the life Elysian
Whose portal we call Death....

And though at times, impetuous with emotion
And anguish long suppressed,
The swelling heart heaves moaning like the ocean
That cannot be at rest.

We will be patient, and assuage the feeling
We may not wholly stay;
By silence sanctifying, not concealing,
The grief that must have way.

HENRY WADSWORTH LONGFELLOW

LOVE IS ENOUGH

Nothing will remove the awful ache, I know. Remember – won't you? – that it is a sign of the success of your relationship with each other. There are so many different kinds of immortality, don't you agree? You now have to look after the part of her which will always be in you, and keep it as she would wish, so that you do for her what she would want to be able to do for herself.

Inevitably there will be things which you will wish had been different. There always are – and I suppose always will be until humanity becomes perfect.

This constant underground worry of "if only I'd done ..." whatever it may be, is an inevitable part of dying for those of us who are left behind. Perhaps what matters is that we can hang on to understanding. The one thing which any genuine love brings is surely that, and I sometimes think it is unfair to the people we have loved and still do, if we assume for them that they would not understand why we did whatever it was. We all muddle on, and only do what we can, and not even always that. But if it is done because of love, then that is enough.

MARGARET J. CHALLIS

THE PROPHET

And a woman spoke, saying, Tell us of Pain. And he said:
  Your pain is the breaking of the shell that encloses your understanding.
  Even as the stone of the fruit must break, that its heart may stand in the sun, so must you know pain.
  And could you keep your heart in wonder at the daily miracles of your life, your pain would not seem less wondrous than your joy;
  And you would accept the seasons of your heart, even as you have always accepted the seasons that pass over your fields.
  And you would watch with serenity through the winters of your grief.
  Much of your pain is self-chosen.
  It is the bitter potion by which the physician within you heals your sick self.
  Therefore trust the physician and drink his remedy in silence and tranquillity:
  For his hand, though heavy and hard, is guided by the tender hand of the Unseen.
  And the cup he brings, though it burn your lips, has been fashioned of the clay which the Potter has moistened with His own sacred tears.

KAHLIL GIBRAN

CONSOLATION WITHOUT GOD

For grief there is no known consolation. It is useless to fill our hearts with bubbles. A loved one gone is gone, and as to the future – even if there is a future – it is unknown. To assure ourselves otherwise is to soothe the mind with illusions; the bitterness of it is inconsolable. The sentiments of trust chipped out on tombstones are touching instances of the innate goodness of the human heart, which naturally longs for good, and sighs itself to sleep in the hope that, if parted, the parting is for the benefit of those that are gone....

The tomb cries aloud to us – its dead silence presses on the drum of the ear like thunder, saying, Look at this and erase your illusions: now know the extreme value of human life; reflect on this and strew human life with flowers; save every hour for the sunshine; let your labour be so ordered that in future times the loved ones may dwell longer with those who love them; open your minds; exalt your souls; widen the sympathies of your hearts; face the things that are now as you will face the reality of death; make joy real now to those you love, and help forward the joy of those yet to be born.

RICHARD JEFFERIES

TO MY FRIEND ON THE DEATH OF HIS SISTER

Thine is a grief, the depth of which another
  May never know;
Yet, o'er the waters, O my stricken brother!
  To thee I go....

I will not mock thee with the poor world's common
  And heartless phrase,
Nor wrong the memory of a sainted woman
  With idle praise.

With silence only as their benediction,
  God's angels come
Where, in the shadow of a great affliction,
  The soul sits dumb!

Yet, would I say what thy own heart approveth:
  Our Father's will,
Calling to Him the dear one whom He loveth,
  Is mercy still.

Not upon thee or thine the solemn angel
  Hath evil wrought:
Her funeral anthem is a glad evangel,
  The good die not!

God calls our loved ones, but we lose not wholly
  What He hath given;
They live on earth, in thought and deed, as truly
  As in His heaven.

And she is with thee; in thy path of trial
  She walketh yet;
Still with the baptism of thy self-denial
  Her locks are wet.

Up then, my brother! Lo, the fields of harvest
  Lie white in view!
She lives and loves thee, and the God thou servest
  To both is true.

JOHN GREENLEAF WHITTIER

SOME THOUGHTS ON LOSS

Our thoughts are with those among the dead into whose sphere we are rising, or who are now rising into our own. Others we inevitably forget, though they be brothers and sisters. Thus the departed may be nearer to us than when they were present. At death, our friends and relatives either draw nearer to us, and are found out, or depart farther from us, and are forgotten. Friends are as often brought near together as separated by death ...

I perceive that we partially die ourselves, through sympathy, at the death of each of our friends or near relatives. Each such experience is an assault on our vital force. It becomes a source of wonder that they who have lost many friends still live. After long watching around the sick-bed of a friend, we too partially give up the ghost with him, and are the less to be identified with this state of things ...

The death of friends should inspire us as much as their lives ...

HENRY DAVID THOREAU

THEY TOLD ME, HERACLITUS

They told me, Heraclitus, they told me you were dead,
They brought me bitter news to hear and bitter tears to shed.
I wept as I remembered how often you and I
Had tired the sun with talking and sent him down the sky.

And now that thou art lying, my dear old Carian guest,
A handful of grey ashes, long, long ago at rest,
Still are thy pleasant voices, thy nightingales, awake;
For Death, he taketh all away, but them he cannot take.

CALLIMACHUS
trans. WILLIAM CORY

IF WE KNEW BUT HOW TO REMEMBER

There would be no difference between the living and the dead if we but knew how to remember. There would be no more dead. The best of what they were dwells with us after fate has taken them from us; all their past is ours; and it is wider than the present, more certain than the future. Material presence is not everything in this world; and we can dispense with it without despairing. We do not mourn those who live in lands which we shall never visit, because we know that it depends on us whether we go to find them. Let it be the same with our dead. Instead of believing that they have disappeared never to return, tell yourselves that they are in a country to which you yourself will assuredly go soon, a country not so far away. And while waiting for the time when you will go there once and for all, you may visit them in thought as easily as if they were still in a region inhabited by the living. The memory of the dead is even more alive than that of the living; it is as though they were assisting our memory, as though they, on their side, were making a mysterious effort to join hands with us on ours. One feels that they are far more powerful than the absent, who continue to breathe as we do.

Try then to recall those whom you have lost, before it is too late, before they have gone too far; and you will see that they will come much closer to your heart, that they will belong to you more truly, that they are as real as when they were in the flesh...

MAURICE MAETERLINCK

PRAYERS ON VISITING A GRAVE

In the quietness of this place I think of her with the love and understanding that still join us together. I remember her goodness and the blessings I received through her. Her memory is precious to me and is always with me.

May her memory continue to strengthen me and guide me. Because life is short, let me fill it with acts of goodness, let me be broader in my sympathies, and purer in my motives.

Help me to learn the meaning and value of life. Help me to know that goodness is not in vain, and the grave is not the end.

As the heavens are high above the earth, so are Your ways beyond man's understanding. Yet Your love surrounds Your children to protect them, for with You are light and comfort and peace.

Amen.

from THE FUNERAL SERVICE OF THE
REFORM SYNAGOGUES OF GREAT BRITAIN

CONTINUITIES

Nothing is ever really lost, or can be lost,
No birth, identity, form – no object of the world,
Nor life, nor force, nor any visible thing;
Appearance must not foil, nor shifted sphere confuse thy
    brain.
Ample are time and space – ample the fields of Nature.
The body, sluggish, aged, cold – the embers left from
    earlier fires,
The light in the eye grown dim, shall duly flame again;
The sun now low in the west rises for mornings and for
    noons continual;
To frozen clods ever the spring's invisible law returns,
With grass and flowers and summer fruits and corn.

WALT WHITMAN

Let me suggest that the bad things that happen to us in our lives do not have a meaning when they happen to us. They do not happen for any good reason which would cause us to accept them willingly. But we can give them a meaning. We can redeem these tragedies from senselessness by imposing meaning on them. The question we should be asking is not, "Why did this happen to me? What did I do to deserve this?" That is really an unanswerable, pointless question. A better question would be, "Now that this has happened to me, what am I going to do about it?"...

We need to get over the questions that focus on the past and on the pain – "why did this happen to me?" – and ask instead the question which opens doors to the future: "Now that this has happened, what shall I do about it?"...

The facts of life and death are neutral. We, by our responses, give suffering either a positive or a negative meaning. Illnesses, accidents, human tragedies kill people. But they do not necessarily kill life or faith. If the death and suffering of someone we love makes us bitter, jealous, against all religion, and incapable of happiness, *we* turn the person who died into one of the 'devil's martyrs'. If suffering and death in someone close to us bring us to explore the limits of our capacity for strength and love and cheerfulness, if it leads us to discover sources of consolation we never knew before, then *we* make the person into a witness for the affirmation of life rather than its rejection.

HAROLD KUSHNER

And then one or other dies. And we think of this as love cut short; like a dance stopped in mid career or a flower with its head unluckily snapped off – something truncated and therefore, lacking its due shape. I wonder. If, as I can't help suspecting, the dead also feel the pains of separation (and this may be one of their purgatorial sufferings), then for both lovers, and for all pairs of lovers without exception, bereavement is a universal and integral part of our experience of love. It follows marriage as normally as marriage follows courtship or as autumn follows summer. It is not a truncation of the process but one of its phases; not the interruption of the dance, but the next figure....

What we want is to live our marriage well and faithfully through that phase too. If it hurts (and it certainly will) we accept the pains as a necessary part of this phase. We don't want to escape them at the price of desertion or divorce ... We will be still married, still in love. Therefore we shall still ache. But we are not at all – if we understand ourselves – seeking the aches for their own sake. The less of them the better, so long as the marriage is preserved. And the more joy there can be in the marriage between the dead and the living, the better.

The better in every way. For, as I have discovered, passionate grief does not link us with the dead but cuts us off from them.

C.S. LEWIS

TREES

O dreamy, gloomy, friendly trees,
I came along your narrow track
To bring my gifts unto your knees
And gifts did you bring back:
For when I brought this heart that burns –
These thoughts that bitterly repine –
And laid them here among the ferns,
And the hum of boughs divine,
Ye vastest breathers of the air,
Shook down with slow and mighty poise
Your coolness on the human care,
Your wonder on its toys,
Your greenness on the heart's despair,
Your darkness on its noise.

HERBERT TRENCH

89

A PRESENCE REMAINING

Parting from the daily sight and touch of dear friends is hard, very hard – but I doubt if after all this parting is so complete as we sometimes think. Who is there who has not felt the presence of one who has departed – a presence remaining still near him for weeks, months and even years, and touching him so nearly that almost the voice could be heard and the form seen? Who is there who has not been conscious of strange intimations thus coming to him as from another world? Does it not seem, after all, that the friend is there, only speaking to our hearts more deeply, more intimately, more tenderly than in ordinary life? ...

And whatever the region to which we pass, Love saves us there, as it does here. It creates a world in which the soul can live and expand in freedom. The ties which bind us together here are not going to be snapt so easily as some of you may think. For indeed, I believe that those who truly love are already twined together in a world far beyond and behind the visible – and in that world they are safe – and their love is safe – from the storms of time and misadventure.

EDWARD CARPENTER

LOVE LIVES BEYOND THE TOMB

Love lives beyond
The tomb, the earth, which fades like dew!
I love the fond,
The faithful, and the true.

Love lives in sleep,
The happiness of healthy dreams:
Eve's dews may weep,
But love delightful seems.

'Tis seen in flowers,
And in the morning's pearly dew;
In earth's green hours,
And in the heaven's eternal blue.

'Tis heard in Spring
When light and sunbeams, warm and kind,
On angel's wing
Bring love and music to the mind ...

Love lives beyond
The tomb, the earth, the flowers, and dew.
I love the fond,
The faithful, young and true.

JOHN CLARE

ACCEPTANCE

When the spent sun throws up its rays on cloud
And goes down burning into the gulf below,
No voice in nature is heard to cry aloud
At what has happened. Birds, at least, must know
It is the change to darkness in the sky.
Murmuring something quiet in her breast,
One bird begins to close a faded eye;
Or overtaken too far from his nest,
Hurrying low above the grove, some waif
Swoops just in time to his remembered tree.
At most he thinks or twitters softly, 'Safe!
Now let the night be dark for all of me.
Let the night be too dark for me to see
Into the future. Let what will be, be.'

ROBERT FROST

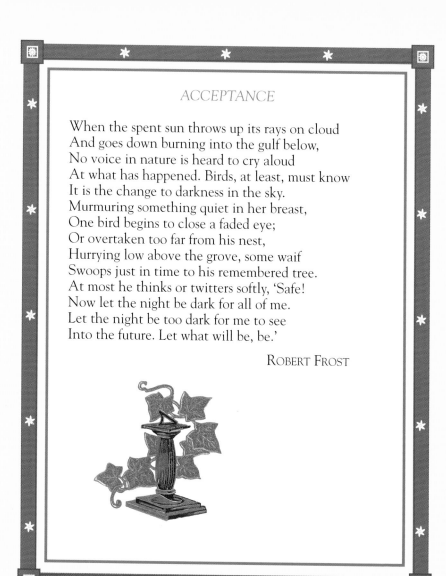

94

Acknowledgements

I have not been able to trace all the copyright holders to reproduce extracts in this book. The publishers will be happy to rectify any omissions in future editions.

I should like to thank the following for permission to reprint:

The British Humanist Association for permission to quote 'If it must be', an anonymous poem which appears in their booklet, *Funerals without God*.

Maria Browne for an extract from a George Macdonald letter.

The estate of Margaret J. Challis for an extract from an unpublished letter written to Celia Haddon.

Jonathan Cape, the Estate of Robert Frost, and Henry Holt and Company Inc. for 'Acceptance' by Robert Frost, from *The Poetry of Robert Frost* edited by Edward Connery Lathem. Copyright 1928, © 1930, 1939, 1949, 1969 by Henry Holt and Co. Inc., reprinted by permission of Henry Holt and Co. Inc.

Faber and Faber for permission to quote 'Stop all the Clocks' from 'Twelve Songs, IX', in *Collected Poems* by W.H. Auden, and for permission to quote two extracts from *A Grief Observed* by C.S. Lewis. Random House Inc. for permission to quote 'Stop all the Clocks' from *W.H. Auden: Collected Poems* by W.H. Auden. Copyright © 1940 and renewed 1968 by W.H. Auden, reprinted by permission of Random House, Inc. HarperCollins, New York, for permission to use extracts from *A Grief Observed* by C.S. Lewis. Copyright © N.W. Clerk, reprinted by permission of HarperCollins Publishers, Inc.

Harvard University Press for Poem 360, 'Death Sets a Thing Significant' by Emily Dickinson, reprinted by permission of the publishers and the Trustees of Amherst College from *The Poems of Emily Dickinson*, Thomas H. Johnson, ed, Cambridge, Mass: The Belknap Press of Harvard University Press. Copyright © 1951, 1955, 1979, 1983 by the President and Fellow of Harvard College.

Kevin Mayhew, for *Do Not Be Afraid* by Gerald Markland. Copyright © Kevin Mayhew Ltd, reproduced by permission, licence number 695120.

Macmillan General Books for permission to quote extracts from *When Bad Things Happen To Good People* by Harold S. Kushner, published by Pan in the UK. Random House Inc for the same extracts: from *When Bad Things Happen To Good People* by Harold S. Kushner. Copyright © 1981, 1989 by Harold S. Kushner. Reprinted by permission of Shocken Books, published by Pantheon Books, a division of Random House Inc.

Random House Inc. for an excerpt from *The Prophet* by Kahlil Gibran. Copyright 1923

Picture Credits

The following illustrations are by Joyce Haddon: **5** *Everlasting Flowers*; **14** *The Beehive in my Garden*; **30** *My Gardening Hat*; **74** *Queen Anne's Lace along the Lane*.

All the following illustrations were supplied by Fine Art Photographic Library Ltd: **8** L. Barzanti, *Roses on a Garden Wall*; **10** John Adams, *Harvesting*; **13** John Waterhouse, *The Annunciation*; **16** Eugene Bidau, *The Wedding Bouquet*; **18** Charles Lutyens, *Cherubs in the Clouds*; **22** Edward Burne-Jones, *The Nymph of the Stars*; **24** Auguste Veillon, *Calm Water*; **27** Benjamin Leader, *An old church with ivy in the grounds of the Duke of Northumberland at Albery*; **28** John Grimshaw, *The Lovers*; **34** Joseph Thors *Autumn in the Woods*; **38** William Blacklock, *By the Fireside*; **42** Carl Aagaard, *A Forest Glade*; **45** James Campbell, *Our Village Clockmaker solving a Problem*; **46** Clarence Roe, *The Waterfall*; **48** Lucien Frank, *In the Orchard*; **51** Joshua Fisher, *A Girl sewing by a Cottage Door*; **53** John Brett, *The Hedger*; **54** James Hill, *A Beautiful Summer's Day*; **57** William Blacklock, *Lunchtime Perparations*; **59** Myles Birket Foster, *Woodland Snowdrops*; **60** Marcus Stone, *His Ship in Sight*; **63** Ivan Aivazosky, *Farewell to the Black Sea*; **64** Arthur Hughes, *Little Lamb who made Thee*; **66** Robert Onderdonk, *Mrs Chandler in her Room*; **69** Albert Goodwin, *Christ in the Garden of Gethsemane*; **70** Daniel Seghers, *A Flower-bedecked Marble Niche containing an Adoration of the Virgin Mary*; **77** Adam Topffer, *An Alpine Landscape*; **78** Alfred Glendening, *A Spring Morning*; **81** Edward Cabot, *A Study of Pink and Yellow Roses*; **82** John Adams, *Surrey Sunset*; **84** W. Scott Myles, *The Butterflies' Haunt*; **89** Edmund Warren, *A Wooded Landscape with Foxgloves*; **91** Richard Redgrave, *The Lovers' Tryst*; **92** Helen Allingham, *Bluebells*.